The Little Adv

The Quest of the Go

by

Stefan Cvetković & Romane Arbogast

Artist:

Stefan Cvetković

(Cover art & Illustrations)

INTRODUCTION

Welcome to this book. We are happy to present to you our work which took our dedication and time but was also a lot of fun to create and put together. We thought about what we would love to read and solve as kids, and just created something that we haven't seen anywhere yet that conjures up mythological elements, storytelling symbolism, activities, and an exciting storyline. In each of us sleeps this adventurer ready to abandon their routine to find a treasure, fight a monster and have his name inscribed in the legend.

We sincerely hope, whether you are a child or a grown up, that you will enjoy the quest and find inspiration.

The solutions to activities and tasks can be found at the end of the book, page 41 if you cannot find the answer by yourself. You can have help from your siblings, your parents or friends, they are of course welcome to join the adventure. The illustrations are in black and white, therefore they are meant to be coloured however you like.

THE LEGEND OF THE GOLDEN APPLE

There was once a tree, far far away, beyond nine seas and nine mountains growing in an evergreen meadow. It was said that every year it would bear a single Golden Apple, shining like the sun, but no one has ever found neither the tree nor the golden apple.

Only the legend tells us, that a dragon steals the sacred fruit, and that one day a brave adventurer would seek and find the apple, taken away by the dragon...

The Wizard Belobrad

« Hey there adventurer ! I can see you are ready to take back the Golden Apple. I can help you with this task...

But let me present myself first, my name is Belobrad I am a wizard and I help the ones which show strength and tenacity. Let me tell you first, that to find this Golden Apple you will have to face multiple challenges, but if you succeed, the apple will be yours, bringing you honour, knowledge and a wonderful gift of memory.»

To win the golden apple you will need four objects :
A *rope*, a *torch*, a *sword* and a *map*.
As you go through the game you will find these objects in your inventory. For now your inventory is empty.

I will give you the *map* and aid you on your quest.
In exchange you will help me create a magical potion for the witch of the forest. If you accept, we will need some plants as well as healing water.

Recipe

Find out the value of each plant, to then find out how many plants You need for the potion!

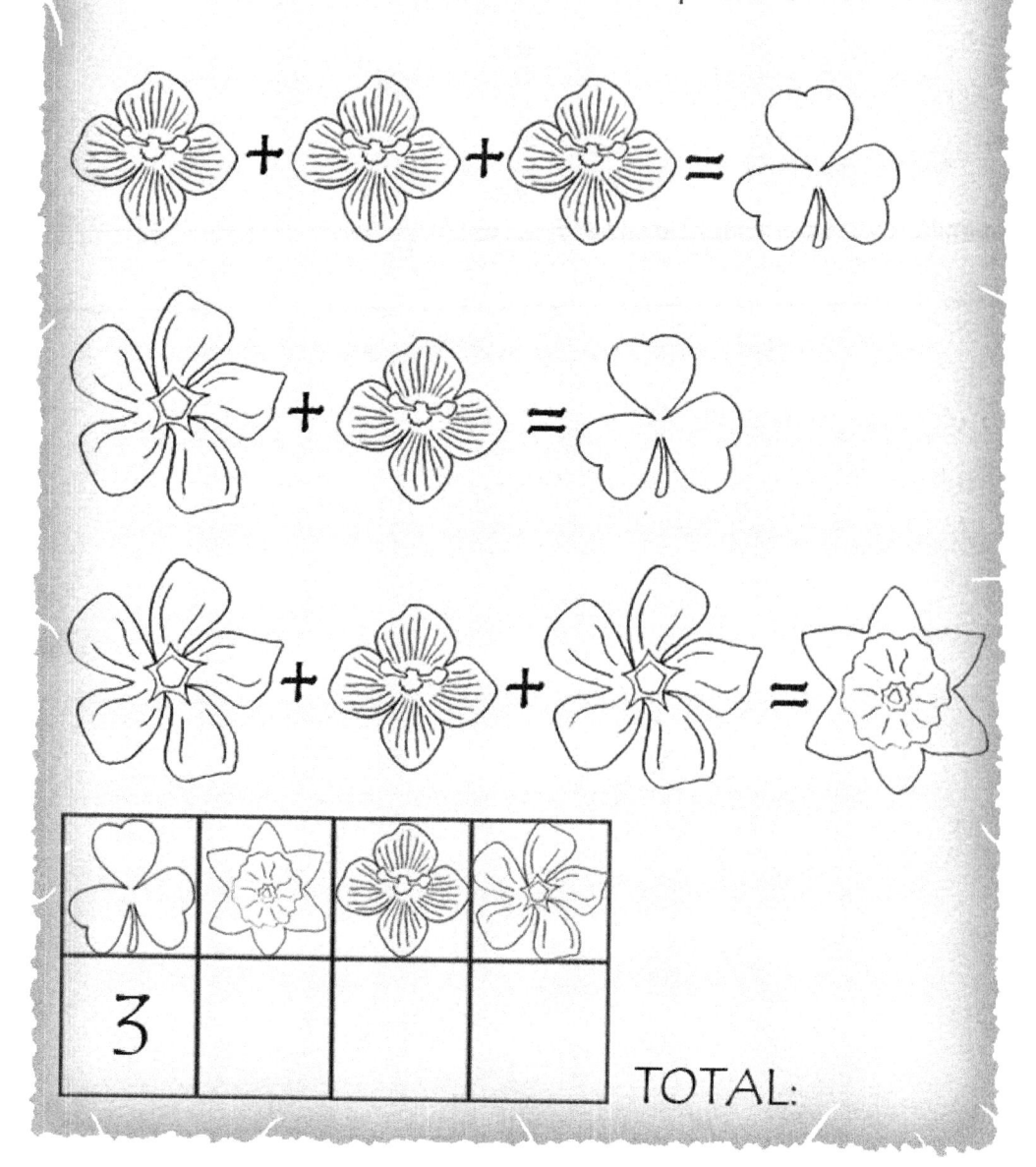

3			

TOTAL:

Link up the dots with a ruler to find the hidden geometric pattern in the plants. Link the last number to the first to finish the shape.

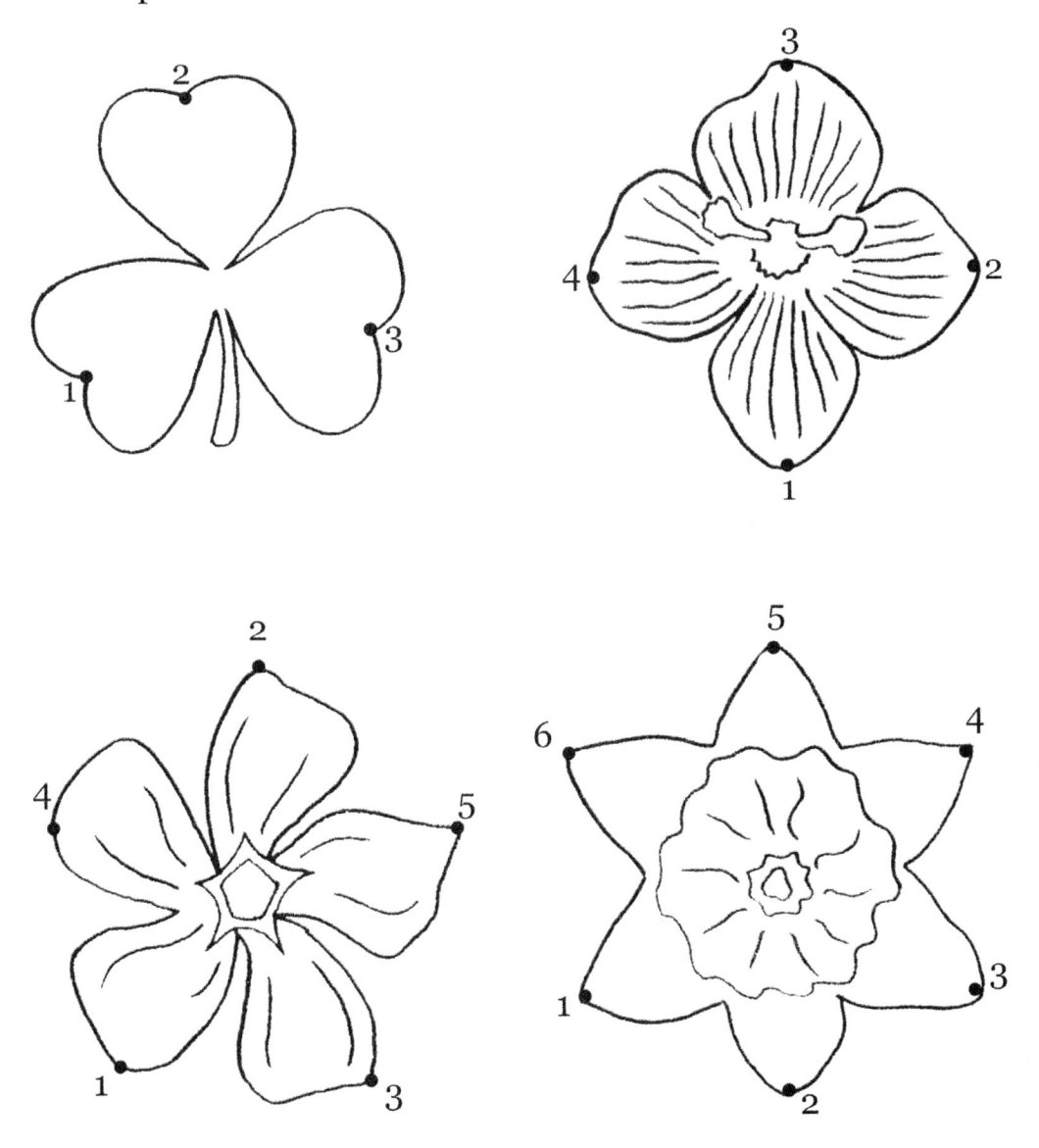

Write the names of the shapes you know under the flowers.

Well done! Thank you for your help. Here is the *map* I promised, and there is a compass on it showing you the directions of the world. Your home is east, between south and east is south-east where the well of Vela is. That is where we are going now. Write the names of the remaining directions on the compass.

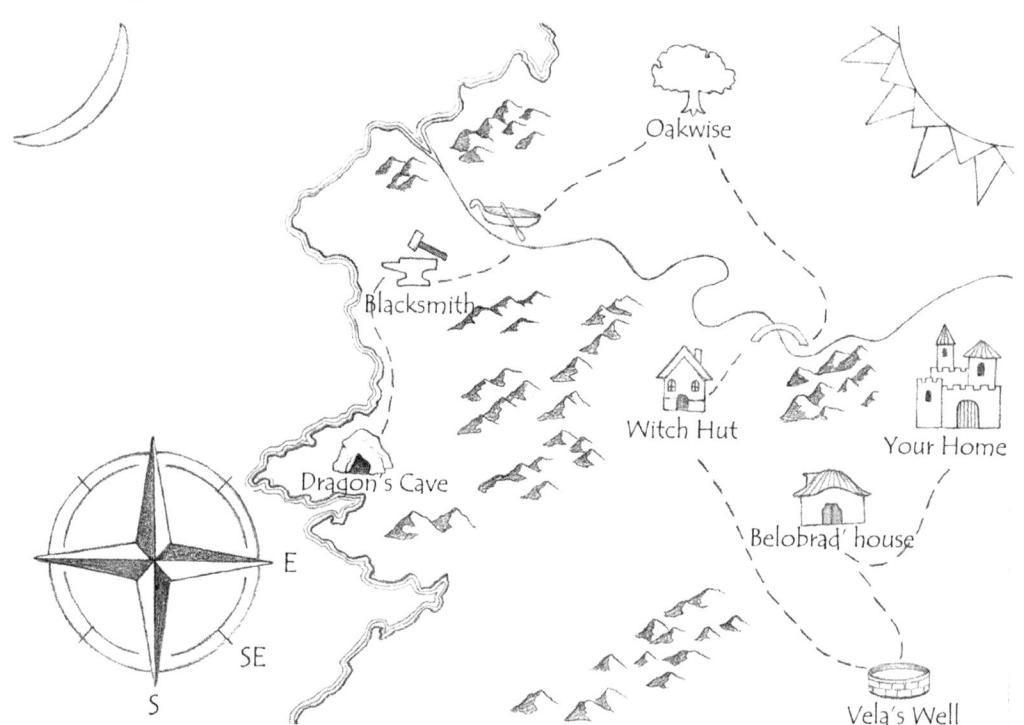

In which direction is the Dragon's Cave?

_____

In which direction is Oakwise?

_____

In which direction is the Blacksmith?

_____

Vela the Fairy

«Welcome to my well. I am Vela, fairy and guardian of the water. Help me remember the names of the inhabitants of my pond, and bring back their colour.»

1._____
2._____
3._____
4._____
5._____

The Pond

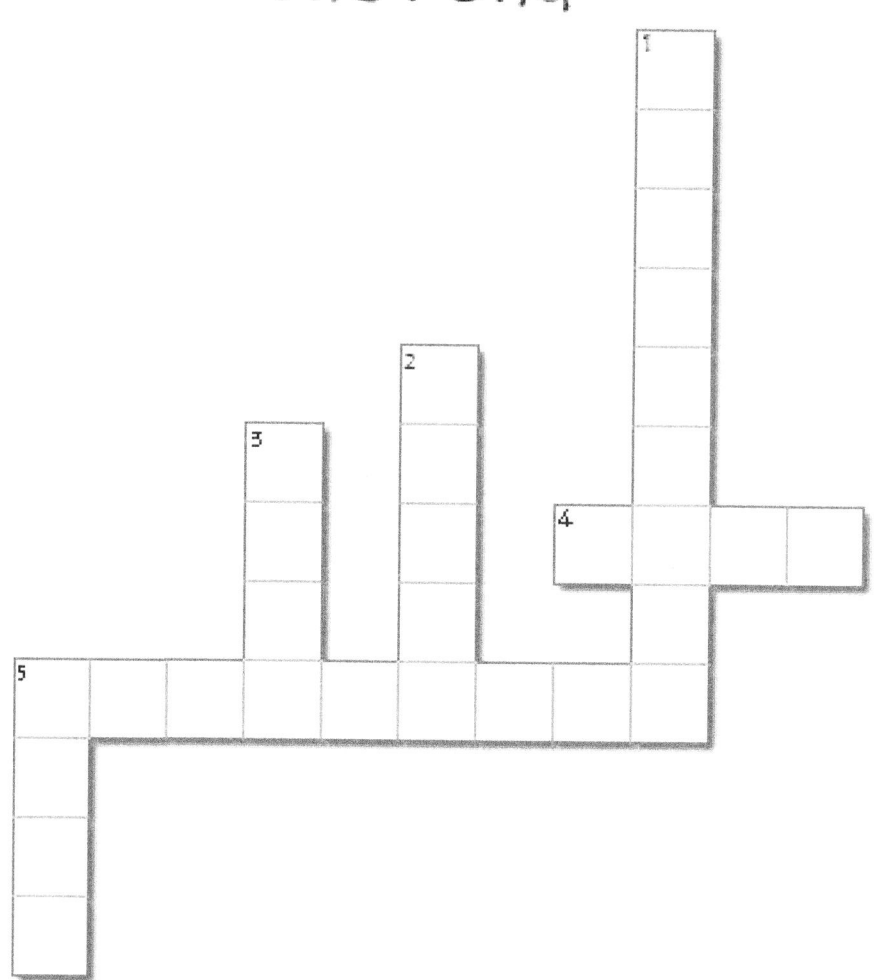

Complete the crossword puzzle!

1. This plant floats on the surface of the water.
2. This bird is tall and gray.
3. It swims in water, it jumps on the ground.
4. It lays eggs and has shiny scales.
5. This insect has four wings.
5. (Down) This bird can fly and swim.

« You did a great job, now I can call all animals and plants of my pond by their name, and so can you!
Here is the well deserved healing water so that Belobrad can make his potion! »

Continue the patterns on Vela's Dress.

« The Witch Hut and Oakwise forest are North from here and you have a long road. Do you know how to find the true north in the night? You don't? It's alright I can teach how to read the map of the stars. There are two constellations which you should find : the Big Bear and its baby, the Little Bear.

The last star of the Little Bear is the Northern Star, follow her and she will always take you to the North.»

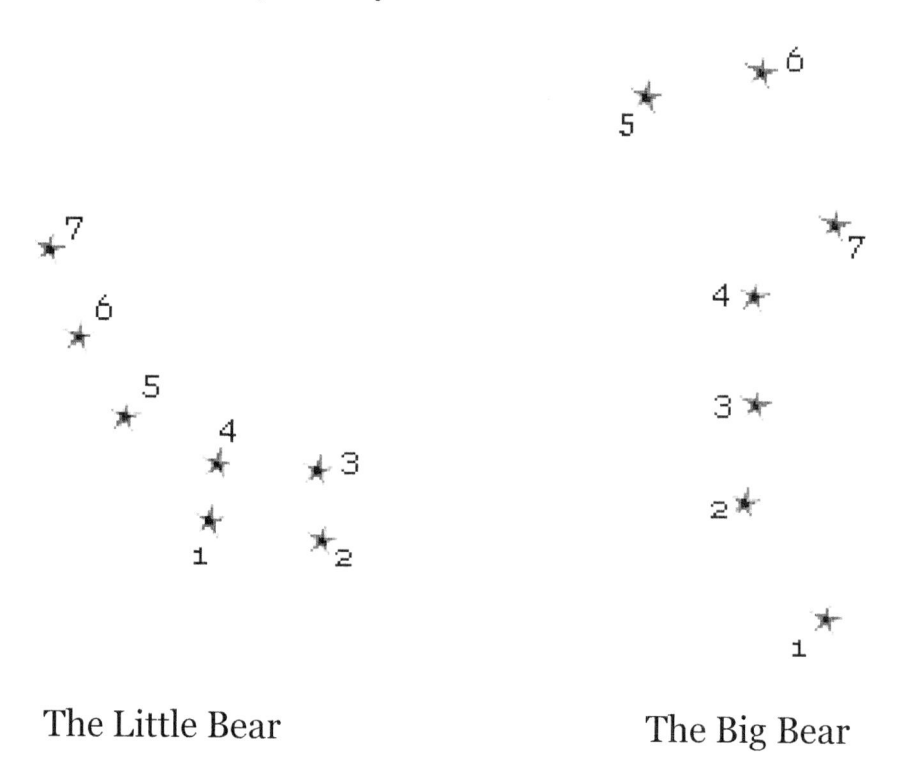

The Little Bear   The Big Bear

Connect the stars in the right order and find the Northern Star.

The Witch

Here is the Witch Hut. Look she has protected her entrance with a spell ! to open the door you will need to **add** one number of each line to arrive at **20**. Not more, not less!

« Hello adventurer, I see you managed to enter the house ! You are a clever spirit. I am the old witch of the forest, but I wasn't always. The dragon which stole the golden apple destroyed half of my house.»

«For your quest to find the Golden Apple I will weave and give you a *rope*, but for that I need your help: Build back the other half of my house which was destroyed.»

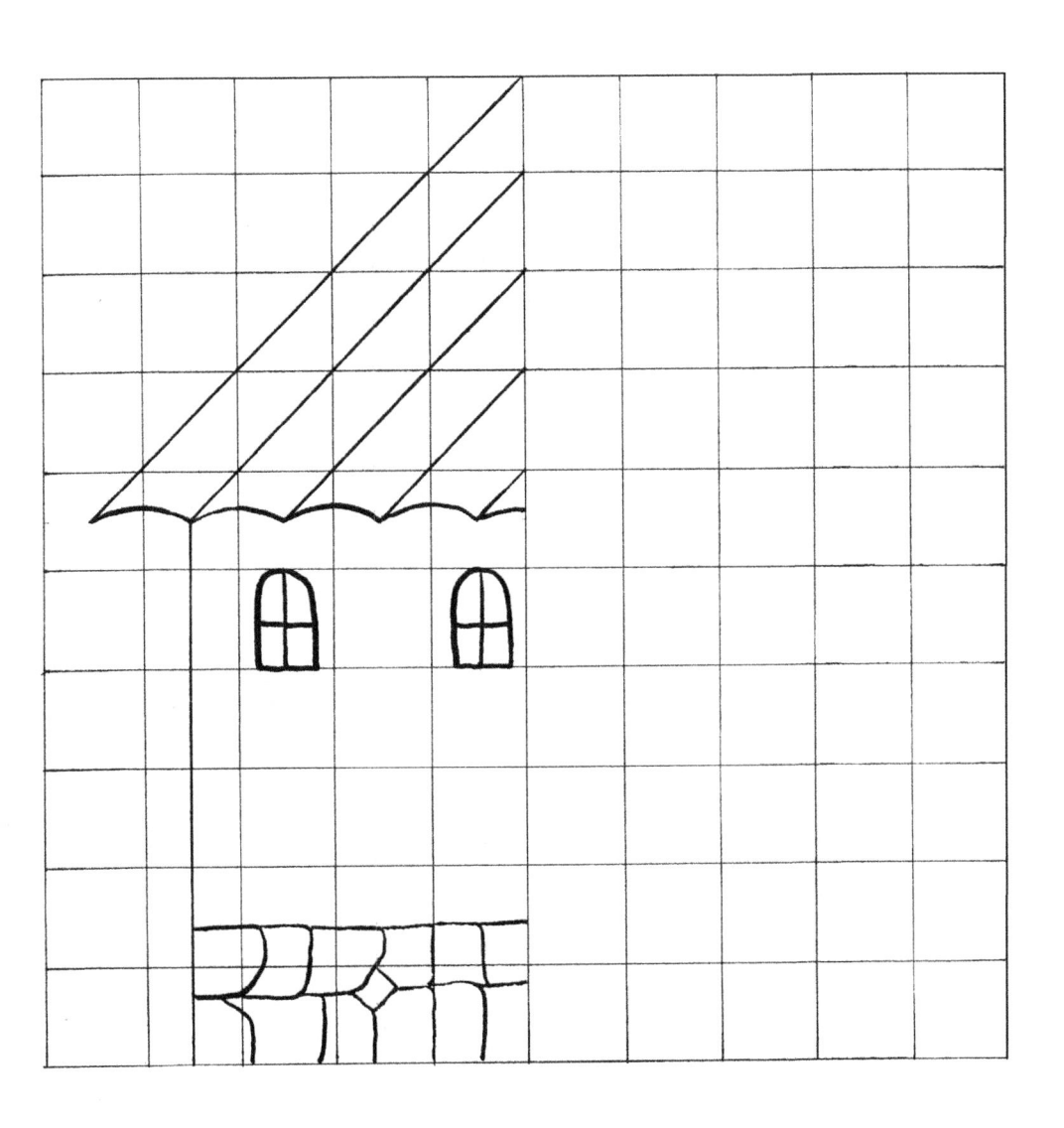

Thank you! Here is your well deserved rope!

Now that we have the 2 first objects we need to find the 2 remaining ones : the *torch* and the *sword*.

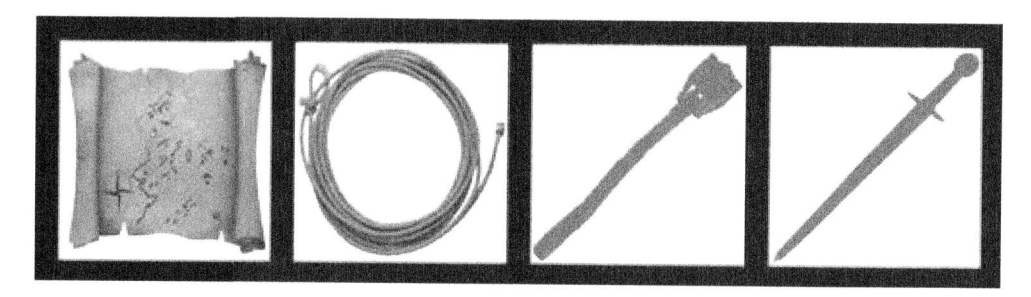

For that we have to cross the river to meet Oakwise. We should get there before nightfall because who knows what dangers await us.

Oh look ! To cross the bridge you will need to **calculate** and go where you are supposed to go. If you calculated right you will cross the bridge successfully.

17	FINISH
16	-5
15	+2
14	-1
13	+2
12	-6
11	-7
10	-5
9	+7
8	+2
7	-5
6	+3
5	+9
4	+4
3	
2	+10
1	4+3

OAKWISE

We passed the bridge, good job! We are now entering the forest to meet Oakwise. Here he is!

«Greetings adventurer, welcome to my forest. I have heard from my birds that you are searching for the Golden Apple. Hidden it is, in the depths of the darkest cave. Indeed a *torch* will be needed to make your way through the darkness.
I can give you fine wood and resin, and in return you will fulfill a few tasks.»

«The first task will be to tell me, if you know, **all the species of birds** living in my branches.»

Do you know which of these birds are migratory?
_____

«Very well! Your next task is to select the correct order representing the cycle of growth of the apple tree.»

Trees and everything else in nature grows following the Fibonacci sequence. It is a very simple mathematical sequence with which we are going to build a tree now.

Each number is the **sum** of the two preceding numbers : ex 1, 2, 3, 5, 8... Calculate the following numbers and continue the tree using this method, then decorate it.

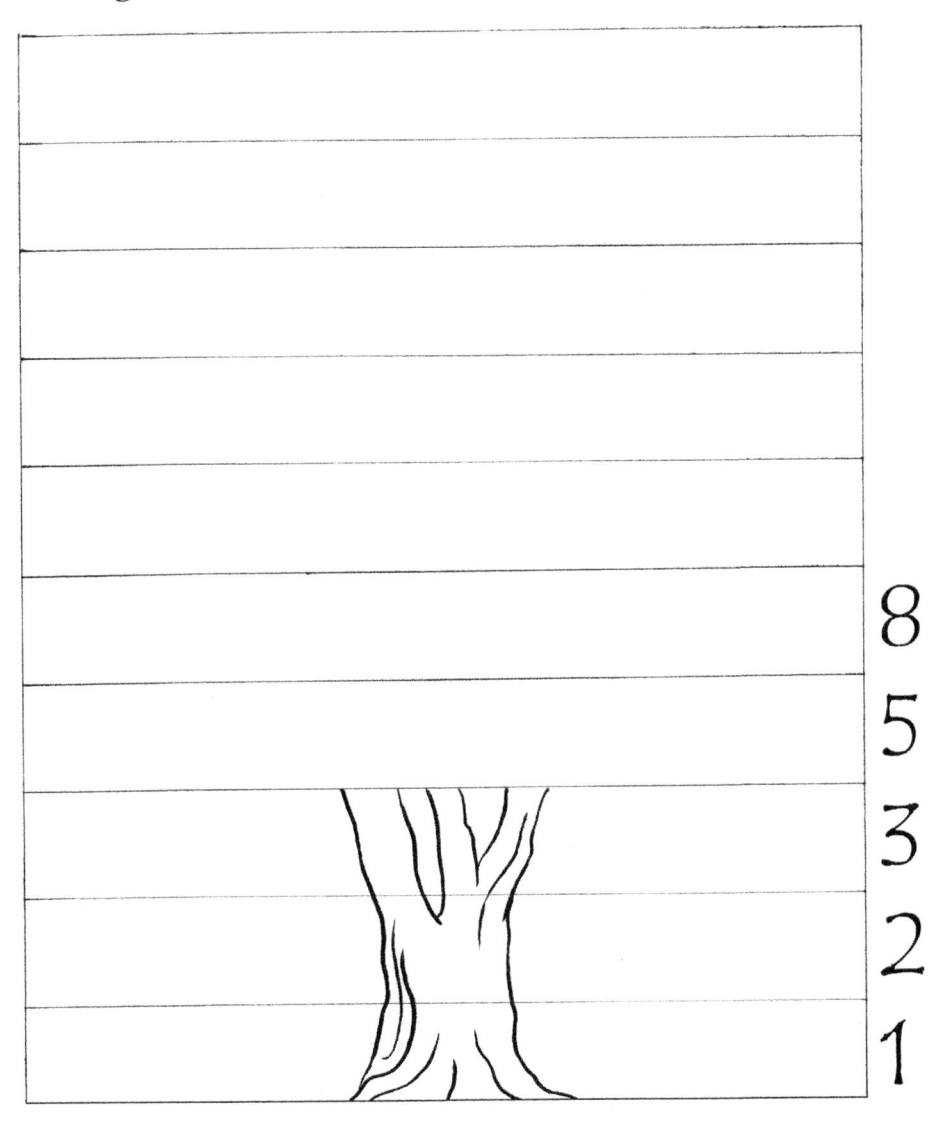

8
5
3
2
1

Congratulations ! This wasn't easy. You have completed the tasks, now you have to **choose** the correct shadow for your *torch*.

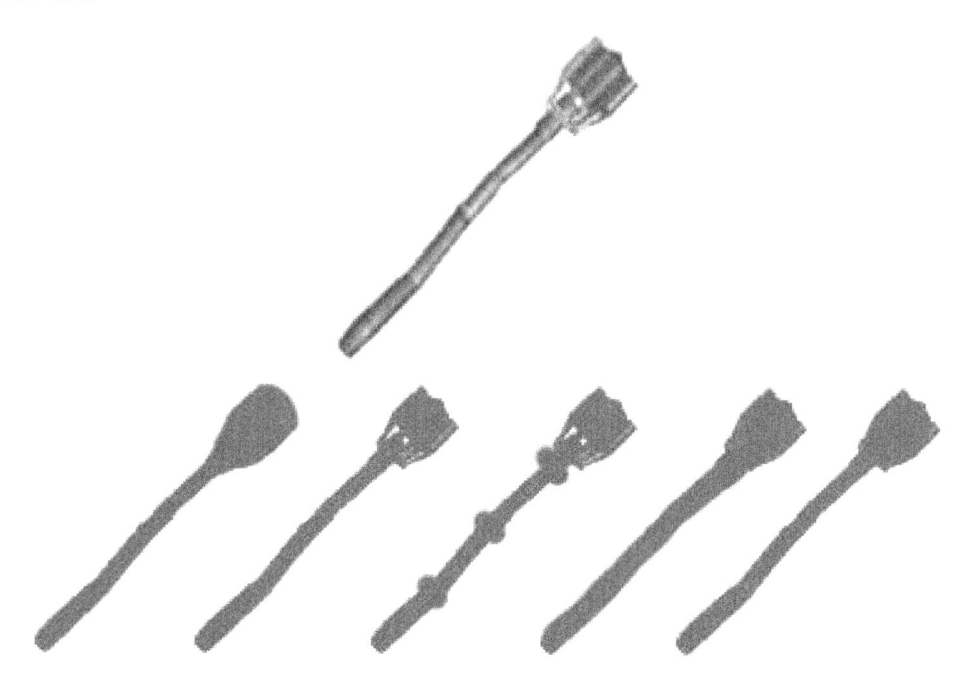

Quickly! We have to go meet the blacksmith, he will help us find the last object!

To reach the blacksmith we need to cross the river again, we will need to take the boat and pay the ferryman. He demands 12 small coins for the journey, but you have one large coin which is worth 25 small ones. He does not look like a trustworthy person. He might want to trick you and pay you back less than he is supposed to. Do you know how many small coins he has to pay you back?

We arrived at the blacksmith's house: to enter we will need to find the right door. To do so, you first have to link the cubes to the shape that corresponds to them, seen from above. The cube corresponds to the grammar form of a word and the shape to the number it is given : its place in the sentence.

You will have to choose, according to the number and the proper grammar, which sentence is the correct one.

The fire
1   2
is alive.
3   4

Lovely is
1   2
the bridge.
3   4

The sword
1   2
was made.
3   4

Adjective   Noun   Verb Present   Definite Article

1   2   3   4

Which door are you going to choose ?

BLACKSMITH

« Who's there? OH! An adventurer! You want to win the Golden Apple? That's brave of you, I wouldn't dare face the dragon! And I don't like darkness... Speaking of darkness I can see you have a *torch*. I can sell you some things that will help you ignite a fire. Here is my shop, you can buy what you need. According to the money you have from the previous adventures, **buy** the two items you need to ignite fire.

Candle - 10 coins; Steel - 7 coins; Flint - 6 coins; Knife - 8 coins; Crystal - 12 coins; Hammer - 11 coins.

« You need my help for the *sword*? No problem. But know that according to the legend, the *sword* has to be made especially for the adventurer which has been chosen to kill the dragon. To make *it* I need my tools. Among them a few objects don't belong : **find** and **circle** them.

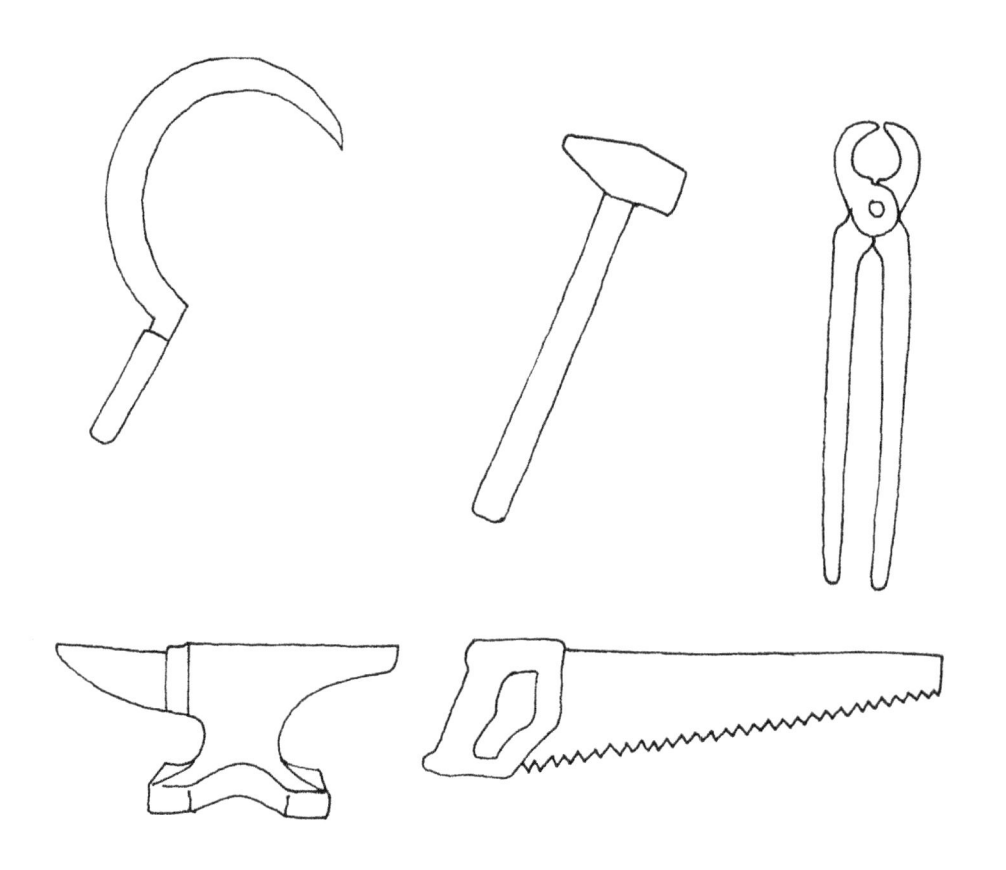

«The *sword* is ready ! Find it among the shades : this will prove if you are worthy of owning the legendary weapon.»

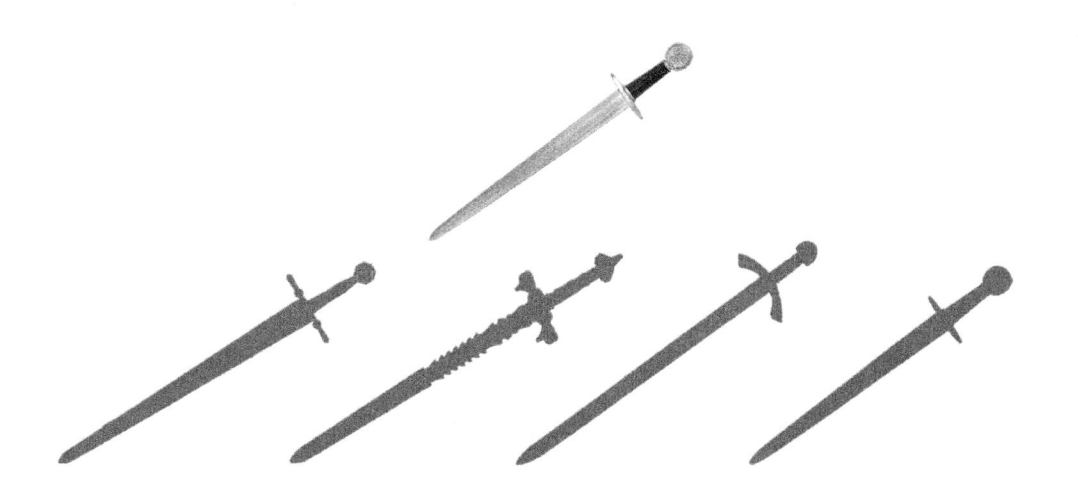

After a long travel, you finally arrive at the entrance of the cave. It looks dark and deep, but you choose not to be scared. You use the *rope*, tie one end around a tree, and the other around your waist, and you slowly descend down into the deep cave. How dark it is here! Thankfully we have a *torch*, and from the blacksmith a *flint* and *steel* to make fire! Look at all these cave paintings, our distant ancestors came here and left us all this beautiful art.

What animals do you see painted ?

_____

ACTIVITIES

Over here, this bull looks lonely :

Thanks to your creativity... Bring him some company.

Look at these hands, they all belong to children. Previous adventurers who came in this cave and left their print on the wall! Leave your handprint on the stone as well, contour it.

Put your hand on the blank page and contour it.

What is this? It looks like a coded message someone engraved on the wall of the cave for a reason, only for a few to decipher it. Let's find out what it means.

[Cipher key:
A B C D E F G H I J
K L M N O P Q R S T
U V W X Y Z]

THE HEARTH THAT WARMS THE WORLD

What is the answer to the riddle ?
_____

The answer will help you solve the next challenge.

Doors! Many of them! How are we going to know which is the right one?

Remember the answer to the riddle.

You chose the correct door, and it led you to a labyrinth! This is the final journey before you face the dragon, whose chamber is at the very centre of the labyrinth. Find your way to the centre of the labyrinth!

THE DRAGON

You have arrived at the dragon's chamber and You are about the engage in battle to win the golden apple, locked inside his chest. In order to defeat the dragon You will need to decrease his energy bar, before he decreases Yours. For this battle You will need a dice, but if You do not have any simply close Your eyes and let your pencil touch a random number in the circle. You have the first move to attack, so roll a dice and write Your result in your «Attack» column. That's Your attack points. Then role again in order to find the defence points of the Dragon, and write the result in his «Defence» column. That's one round. The next round the Dragon will have the first attack move, and so forth. If the attack points are higher than the defence points, then damage has been made. If the defence is higher than the attack, then no damage has been made. For example, if the dice roll gives You 5 attack points, and 3 defence points to the Dragon, then You have made damage of 2 energy points (5-3=2). If the Dragon's attack is 3, and Your defence is 5, then no damage has been made. Each of you has ten points in the energy bar, colour the energy points in Yours or the Dragon's energy bar each time damage has been made, until the bar is completely coloured, indicating one's death.

If You lose, simply try again! Good luck!

You

Dragon

1 3
4 5
2 6

YOU		DRAGON	
ATTACK	DEFENCE	ATTACK	DEFENCE

You have defeated the Dragon and successfully completed the quest of the Golden Apple!

Congratulations!

Solutions:

1. Recipe: 1 + 1 + 1 = 3; 2 + 1 = 3; 2 + 1 + 2 = 5
TOTAL: 11 (3 + 5 + 1 + 2)

2. Geometric shapes of flowers: Triangle, Rhombus, Pentagram (star), Hexagon (6 sided polygon).

3. The missing directions on the compass are Southwest (SW), West (W), Northwest (NW), North (N) Northeast (NE).
In which direction is the Dragon's Cave?
  West.
In which direction is Oakwise?
  North.
In which direction is the Blacksmith?
  North/ Northwest.

4. The names of the animals in Vela's pond: 1. Heron; 2. Fish; 3. Frog; 4. Duck; 5. Dragonfly.
  «The Pond» crossword puzzle: 1. Waterlily; 2. Heron; 3. Frog; 4. Fish; 5. Dragonfly; 5. (Down) Duck.

5. The entrance of the Witch's house

First possibility : 1 + 2 + 5 + 2 + 10 = 20

Second possibility : 7 + 4 + 5 + 2 + 2 = 20

6. Calculating to cross the bridge

Tiles order: 1; 7; 2; 12; 6; 9; 16; 11; 4; 8; 10; 5; 14; 13; 15; 17

7. Species of birds living in the branches of Oakwise :

The woodpecker, the sparrow, the eagle, the owl, the swallow, the turtledove (not the pigeon !)

Which bird is migrating ?

-Some eagles migrate, some don't.

-Swallows migrate to Africa around September. They can travel up to 10 000km to reach their winter destination.

-Turtledoves migrate to the Sahara.

8. The cycle of the apple tree :

First the seed, then the sprout, the tree, the flower and the fruit.

It is important to remember that it is a cycle, not a timeline. We cannot answer this question : what came first, the tree or the seed? Everything comes back as a cycle, the cycle of life.

9. The tree branches off following the Fibonacci sequence: 1, 2, 3, 5, 8, 13, 21, 34, 55, 89...

10. Find the correct shadow of the torch: It's the second one from the left.

11. Crossing the river: The ferryman needs to pay you back 13 small coins. 25 - 12 = 13

12. Blacksmith's doors :
adjective - 4; Noun - 2; Verb present - 3 ; Definite article - 1
The correct sentence is then : «The fire is alive.»
Therefore you should choose the first door.

13. The Blacksmith: You have 13 coins left, and from the blacksmith you need to buy a flint and a steel, which in total cost exactly 13 coins.

14. The Blacksmith's tools: The blacksmith does not need a saw and a sickle to forge you a sword.

15. The shadows of the sword: The correct shadow is the first on the right.

16. The animals painted in the walls of the cave are: Bulls (Aurochs), Horses and Deer.

17. The riddle: The coded riddle is «The hearth that warms the world» and the answer to the riddle is «the sun».

18. Many doors: Select the door with the sun. It will lead you to the labyrinth where the dragon lives.